KT-230-308

To Frankie

Love from Frankie

LADYBIRD BOOKS
UK | USA | Canada | Ireland | Australia
India | New Zealand | South Africa

Ladybird Books is part of the Penguin Random House group of companies
whose addresses can be found at global.penguinrandomhouse.com.
ladybird.com

 Penguin
Random House
UK

First published 2016
001

Printed in China

A CIP catalogue record for this book is available from the British Library

ISBN: 978-0-241-24988-8

Daddy Pig's
Words of Wisdom

Being a dad is as easy as eating chocolate cake. I would know, I am a bit of an expert at it, after all.

Here are my top tips on being one of the
world's greatest dads . . .

But Daddy,
dinner's ready!

Firstly, us dads always like to get up bright and early, ready for a fun-filled day with the little ones.

It's best to leave breakfast to us.
We'll show everyone
how it's done . . .

. . . and make them smile.

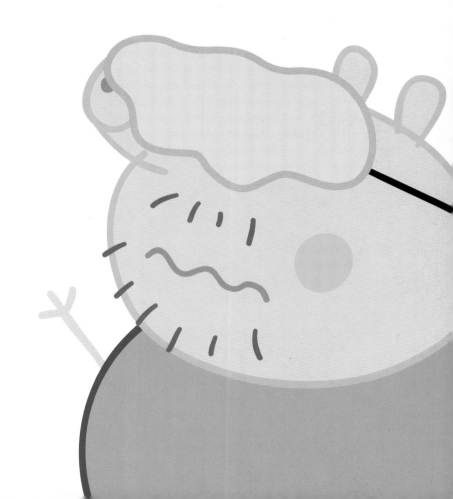

Entertaining the children is a doddle.

We can do it standing on one leg . . .

. . . or even lying down.

When it comes to

DIY,

everyone should stand back
and watch us craftsmen at work.

And when it comes to going for
a drive, there are two rules:

Rule 1. A dad always **looks** like
he knows what he's doing.

Rule 2. A dad **never** admits
that he might be a bit lost.

The great outdoors is the perfect place to display an expert dad's natural athletic ability . . .

Huff, puff!

... and his **superb** survival skills.

I must say, sometimes even expert dads
need to read the instructions . . .

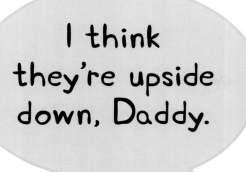

. . . But most things come
naturally, like showing everyone how
champions
like to do things.

We're a
bit muddy,
Daddy.

Dads also do
a **great** job
of cleaning up.

Finally, when it comes to bedtime, us dads have it **all** under control.

Our **expert** story-reading skills will
send the little ones straight to . . .

Sometimes even the greatest expert daddies need to take a little nap.

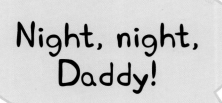

Night, night, Daddy!